Secrets of
Highly Effective
Meetings

The Practicing Administrator's Leadership Series
Jerry J. Herman and Janice L. Herman, Editors

ROADMAPS
TO SUCCESS

Other Titles in This Series Include:

The Path to School Leadership: A Portable Mentor
Lee G. Bolman and Terrence E. Deal

Holistic Quality: Managing, Restructuring, and Empowering Schools
Jerry J. Herman

Selecting, Managing, and Marketing Technologies
Jamieson A. McKenzie

Individuals With Disabilities: Implementing the Newest Laws
Patricia F. First and Joan L. Curcio

Violence in the Schools: How to Proactively Prevent and Defuse It
Joan L. Curcio and Patricia F. First

Women in Administration: Facilitators for Change
L. Nan Restine

Power Learning in the Classroom
Jamieson A. McKenzie

Computers: Literacy and Learning
A Primer for Administrators
George E. Marsh II

Restructuring Schools: Doing It Right
Mike M. Milstein

Reporting Child Abuse:
A Guide to Mandatory Requirements for School Personnel
Karen L. Michaelis

Handbook on Gangs in Schools:
Strategies to Reduce Gang-Related Activities
Shirley R. Lal, Dhyan Lal, and Charles M. Achilles

Conflict Resolution: Building Bridges
Neil H. Katz and John W. Lawyer

Resolving Conflict Successfully: Needed Knowledge and Skills
Neil H. Katz and John W.Lawyer

Secrets of Highly Effective Meetings

Maria M. Shelton
Laurie K. Bauer

CORWIN PRESS, INC.
A Sage Publications Company
Thousand Oaks, California

For information address:

Corwin Press, Inc.
A Sage Publications Company
2455 Teller Road
Thousand Oaks, California 91320

SAGE Publications Ltd.
6 Bonhill Street
London EC2A 4PU
United Kingdom

SAGE Publications India Pvt. Ltd.
M-32 Market
Greater Kailash I
New Delhi 110 048 India

Printed in the United States of America

Library of Congress Cataloging-in-Publication Data

Shelton, Maria M.
    Secrets of highly effective meetings / Maria M. Shelton,
Laurie K. Bauer.
        p.   cm. — (Roadmaps to success)
    Includes bibliographical references.
    ISBN 0–8039–6133–2 (pbk.)
        1. Meetings.   I. Bauer, Laurie K.   II. Title.   III. Series.
HF5734.5.S53   1994
658.4'56—dc20   93–40542

94 95 96 97 98 10 9 8 7 6 5 4 3 2 1

Corwin Press Production Editor: S. Marlene Head

Contents

Foreword

Attending meetings is a frequent fact of life for everyone in education. Occasionally a meeting is well-planned, well-run, and productive. But all too often meetings are poorly planned, do not deal with the important matters at hand, and—when they're over—prove to have been a waste of time.

In *Secrets of Highly Effective Meetings*, Maria Shelton and Laurie Bauer provide a wealth of information that can make your meetings more efficient and effective. They outline (1) the correlation between excellent meetings and excellent results; (2) how to plan for, open, conduct, and follow through with meetings; and (3) strategies for managing problems that arise during meetings.

A series of Resources provides helpful ideas and models for optimum planning and conducting of efficient, effective meetings. The Annotated Bibliography and References section at the end of the book is a useful source for those who wish to pursue the topic in more depth.

If you are responsible for planning or conducting meetings—or if you simply want to know how to become a more productive meeting participant—you will find *Secrets of Highly Effective Meetings* an indispensable guidebook.

JERRY J. HERMAN
JANICE L. HERMAN
Series Co-Editors

About the Authors

Maria M. Shelton is Director of the Ed.D. Program for Educational Leaders at Nova Southeastern University, Fort Lauderdale, Florida. She received her doctorate from Texas A&M University where she majored in educational leadership and minored in curriculum and instruction. Her dissertation on "Conducting and Evaluating Meetings" eventually resulted in the publication of *Faculty Meeting Leader's Guide* (Baker & Barnett Publishing).

For innovations in teaching, Maria Shelton was honored by *Texas Woman's Magazine* and was recognized by the governor of Michigan as one of the top two professors at Central Michigan University. She serves as president of Professors of Elementary and Middle School Administrators, under the auspices of the National Association of Elementary School Principals, and is president-elect of the National Council of Professors of Educational Administration.

Shelton's leadership experience in public schools, corporate sectors, and higher education has provided her with rich, diverse environments for exploring ways to make meetings effective and morale-enhancing. In addition, she conducts extensive training for leaders in both private and public sectors on planning, chairing, and evaluating meetings.

Laurie K. Bauer is currently Principal of Schulenburg High School in Schulenburg, Texas. She received her bachelor's degree in zoology from Texas A&M University, her master's degree in chemistry education from the University of Southern Mississippi, and her doctorate in administration and instructional leadership from the University of Alabama.

Laurie Bauer's 16 years of teaching experience in chemistry and physics have been recognized as exemplary in three different states. She has received the state Presidential Awards in both Texas and Mississippi and was inducted into the Alabama Teacher Hall of Fame. She has presented numerous workshops and meetings on effective teaching strategies. In addition, she has implemented many innovative programs in secondary schools by successfully orchestrating highly effective meetings.

Introduction

Many educators consider school meetings to be giant time killers and of little value. However, people who lead meetings generally think that they are effective *and* meaningful. The truth probably lies somewhere in between. If meetings *are* to be useful, then meaningful interaction must occur, and for that to happen, we—as school leaders—must practice effective facilitation skills. We must operate differently than we have in the past to meet the challenges of schooling America's children.

Secrets of Highly Effective Meetings provides the educational leader with practical, hands-on strategies for improving meetings. Chapter 1, "Benefits of Productive Meetings," addresses how morale, culture, planning, team building, and change are enhanced through productive meetings. Chapter 2, "Types of Meetings," examines different meetings in which school leaders participate: parent, faculty, grievance, community groups, media, student, and opening and closing of school. Chapter 3, "How to Plan Successful Meetings," stresses the importance of determining if a meeting is necessary and, if it is, establishing the purpose, agenda, handouts, time, site, participants, and minutes. Chapter 4, "Opening and Closing Meetings Effectively," discusses the leader's role in terms of establishing climate, facilitating the group, observing body language, building consensus, closing, evaluating, and acting on evaluations. Chapter 5, "Managing Conflict in Meetings," analyzes conflict that frequently occurs in meetings and illustrates ways to handle it. The Resources offer a plethora of examples for use in planning, chairing, and evaluating meetings. A pretest is included to determine how well the reader is doing with meetings. Finally, the Annotated Bibliography and References provide additional sources for information on meetings.

All in all, *Secrets of Highly Effective Meetings* is a *must* for today's educational leader who faces an increasingly difficult job—establishing, shaping, and implementing vision in the 21st-century school.

Benefits of Productive Meetings

Although many educators, from long experience, have negative perceptions of meetings, it *is* possible to organize highly successful and productive meetings. De Bruyn and Benjamin (1983) emphasize that positive perceptions of meeting are possible: "In truth, people do like good meetings. They love important ones, and feel more significant about themselves when they've attended a productive meeting. They enjoy telling other people about the big or exclusive meetings they attend . . . . Remember, people are social beings. They are not loners. They want to come together" (p. 10).

Personal, conversational meetings are usually preferred over those with formal, "I'm-in-control"-type formats. Participants interact more often when they are face-to-face and when they are treated as equals. Inviting only those people who are directly involved with the meeting's primary issue of concern, rather than requiring all staff members to attend, also helps improve staff perceptions of meetings.

Well-run meetings generate the following positive outcomes: high morale, culture development, a clear vision of the future, team building, and change facilitation.

High Morale

High morale is achieved primarily through leader-staff communication. In fact, communicating is probably the most important thing a leader does (Shelton, 1989). Elaborating on the importance of communication, Nigro (1984) states that a leader's chief responsibility is to establish, maintain, and work on communication with staff. An effective leader justifies and explains "what is coming down the pipeline." When staff is aware of what is going on, they feel that they are part of the organization and that they have something to contribute. Staff members are also much more productive and supportive when the leader informs the staff about what is happening and secures their input on identifying and solving problems.

Culture Development

In the context of meetings, culture may be defined as having the following elements: values (basic beliefs), heroes (who personify the culture), rules and rituals (expected behaviors), and network (storytellers, spies, priests, cabals, and whisperers) (Deal & Kennedy, 1982). In their book, *Corporate Cultures: The Rites and Rules of Corporate Life*, Deal and Kennedy (1982) note that "the most important management ritual continues to be the formal meeting . . . some companies require many; in others, it is a real breakthrough to get everyone to sit down to one meeting a month" (p. 70).

Values constitute the heart of the culture, and these are often transmitted through meetings. In fact, the leader models values when chairing and participating in meetings. By observing leader and hero behaviors, staff members see and learn what is expected in terms of dress, language, behavior, communication, ceremonies, conflict, and stories. Meetings provide new employees with the opportunity to learn what it takes to succeed in the organization. Newcomers and staff members who fail to observe and therefore fail to learn the culture simply won't succeed.

Clear Vision of the Future

Covey (1992) stresses in *The 7 Habits of Highly Effective People* the need for leaders to be "proactive." Certainly, through meetings, the leader asks, "Where are we?" "Where do we want to go?" "How will we know when we get there?" The proactive leader climbs the tallest tree and yells, "Wrong jungle"; the reactive leader yells, "Shut up, we're making progress." Basically, the leader helps the organization know where it is and where it needs to go; with this information, tactical and strategic planning can begin.

Team Building

Truly, the "whole is greater than the parts" (Covey, 1992, p. 26); today, a leader can no longer lead by being a "one-person show." For this reason, it is important that the leader encourage active involvement of staff members in problem identification and in problem solving, crucial components of planning for the future. But teams don't just happen; over time they evolve through common experiences and challenges. Individuals bond into teams because there is something in it for them. Being part of a "winning" team increases the members' self-esteem and commitment to the organization, both of which are vital to organizational culture.

Helping to identify and solve problems allows staff members to feel they are "trusted" by the leader. When trust has been established between the leader and staff persons, the staff will be more likely to live up to their potential. Often staff members are the ones who best understand the problem and can offer the best possible solution. An involved staff will tend to "own" the solution and want to make it work.

If agreement cannot readily be reached on a solution, try to arrange consensus, rather than voting. With voting, one group "wins" and the other group "loses." With consensus, everyone "wins." Obviously, negotiating a consensus requires more time than voting, but the goal is to reach a solution that everyone buys into and owns. Consensus building is also an excellent opportunity to model patience, humor, respect, and vision, which in turn reinforces a positive culture.

Usually the major barrier to effective problem solving is not in finding a solution, but rather in failing to first adequately define the problem. Many times people jump right in and describe the symptoms of the problem without defining what the problem is. In the meeting setting, the leader guides participants in the important step of framing the problem in terms of who, what, when, where, why, and how.

Once the problem is defined, the next step is active brainstorming. Here the task is to generate a large number of possible solutions without censorship or criticism. Brainstorming can be done in one of several ways: 1) Have someone write ideas on a flip chart as group members spontaneously give them; 2) Go around the table, and have each person offer an idea in turn (this will give them more time on their responses); 3) Use computers and give each person 30 minutes to type in as many solutions as possible without interruptions from others; 4) Use E-mail to conduct the meeting so that people can stay in their offices instead of traveling to another site; 5) Begin the meeting with a phrase like, "I know it sounds crazy, but why couldn't we . . . ?" Regardless of which brainstorming technique is used, encourage lots of ideas.

After brainstorming, evaluate each idea on the basis of its weaknesses and strengths. Then compare, weed, and discard them until only the best solution remains or is obvious to everyone. At this stage, try to prevent "verbal locks on creativity" such as: 1) "We've always done it this way"; 2) "That won't work"; and 3) "At _____, we did it this way." Make it clear up front that history is irrelevant and that everyone must focus on reaching the best solutions today.

Through the medium of meetings, the proactive leader nurtures and reinforces team work and ensures that time is set aside for the team to play together, as well as work together. In the meeting setting, the leader can also evaluate where the team is in terms of morale, values, concerns, and challenges.

Change Facilitation

Change is difficult in the best of circumstances. Many people are threatened by change because they don't know what to expect. Their worst fears may materialize. They may lose control. They may lose their job. However, change is inevitable and necessary for organizational as well as personal growth. When staff members have input into change and are encouraged to work together toward clear-cut goals, rather than merely being told what is coming down, they feel more comfortable and secure. Consensus building greatly facilitates the change process by giving individuals a sense of control over what takes place in the group.

In sum, through meetings a leader builds morale by improving communication with the staff; enhances culture by modeling what it takes to succeed in the organization; plans for the future by determining where the organization is and where it needs to go and by identifying, brainstorming, and solving problems; builds teams by encouraging common experiences and by collectively facing challenges; and facilitates change by getting people to agree on the changes that will occur.

Types of Meetings

In the business of education, meetings are a way of life. It is standard operating procedure to have some type of meeting daily. We thrive on meetings. Our daily schedule is dictated by meetings. When we are in meetings we are "on stage." How we as leaders conduct our meetings determines other peoples' perception of our business.

All meetings, whether planned or unplanned, have the same four elements:

1. Program—commonly called the agenda—stated or hidden
2. Players—those involved in the production
3. Production—purpose of the meeting
4. Preparation—readiness degree of the leader to handle the meeting

Planned Meetings

Planned meetings are easier to handle than unplanned meetings because we can prepare ahead of time for them. Types of planned meetings include some parent-teacher conferences, faculty meetings, special education meetings called ARD's (Admission, Review, and Dismissal), union grievance meetings, community meetings, and opening and closing school meetings.

The next section describes planned meetings and how we as leaders can prepare ourselves for these meetings.

Parent-Teacher Conferences

Parent-teacher conferences are usually scheduled with some specific purpose in mind. The meeting may be generated by the teacher or by the parent(s) but is almost never requested by the student. Most students really don't want their parent(s) at the school anyway. Parents who ask to meet with their child's teacher are generally concerned about some aspect of the education business including its employees. The parent-teacher meeting is usually focused on how to improve the student's performance or behavior in class.

Prepare for planned parent meetings by gathering all the information available that pertains to the student involved. As a rule of thumb, whoever calls the meeting starts the meeting.

Other helpful hints include the following:

1. Listen intently, making eye contact at all times.
2. Avoid sitting behind your desk. Choose instead a round table or side-by-side chairs.
3. Stop all incoming calls, unless they are emergencies.
4. Try to have the student's other teacher(s) attend.
5. If possible, allow the student to attend the meeting.
6. Keep the lines of communication open. Never let the parent(s) leave the office angry.
7. During the discussion, emphasize at least two positive traits in the student and one positive parenting trait that you have observed.
8. Restate the problem and the agreed-on solution before ending the meeting, including everyone's role in arriving at the solution.

One of our mentor teachers once said, "Always let parents leave a conference feeling good about themselves with hope for their child." It may be difficult at times to reach this goal; however, it is attainable through active preparation and communication.

Faculty Meetings

Another type of planned meeting is the staff or faculty meeting. The faculty meeting is generally attended by all employees directly related to and/or impacted by the purpose of the meeting. These may include all staff members—including teachers, other administrators, custodians, paraprofessionals, and cafeteria employees—or only certain groups or departments. Most faculty meetings are called for the purpose of implementing and/or making changes in administrative policies or directives, or to analyze and improve overall student achievement.

Faculty meetings actually begin when the agenda is mailed out to players. Always give advance notice for staff meetings. Generally, one work week is adequate advance notice; however, meetings scheduled outside the workday should be announced at least two weeks in advance so that the necessary arrangements can be made. Check activity calendars to avoid conflicts. Whenever possible, schedule meetings within the workday, because meetings scheduled outside the workday may be more difficult for employees to attend due to other commitments. Do not announce meetings with the proviso "If you can not attend, please see me." Assume that all players will attend. Handle individual attendance problems as they arise.

A copy of the agenda should be mailed or delivered to every person who is expected to attend. It should *not* be posted in the teacher's lounge or tacked to the bathroom door. If the meeting is important enough to call, it is important enough to make sure each person involved receives an announcement. A meeting announcement using invitation format encourages participation. You decide which of the following notices sounds better:

THERE WILL BE A FACULTY MEETING . . .
or
YOU ARE INVITED TO ATTEND THE FACULTY MEETING . . .

or

YOU SHALL ATTEND THE FACULTY MEETING SCHEDULED
FOR . . .

The first notice indicates only that a faculty meeting is planned
but does not indicate that attendance is expected. The second notice politely requests the recipient's attendance. The third notice is
a command. The second notice is a clear choice because people
respond more positively to an invitation than to a command (See
Resource A: Invitation to Attend).

Special Education Meetings

Special education meetings, commonly called ARD's (Admission,
Review, and Dismissal) are planned meetings. An ARD meeting is
most often called to formally determine the appropriate educational
setting and develop or modify an individual education plan (IEP)
for a student. Participants of these meetings may include a diag-
nostician, the student's regular classroom teacher, a special education
teacher, an administrator, the parent(s), and sometimes the student.
Occasionally, the presence of a physician, therapist, or psycholo-
gist is also required to provide relevant information.

Some ARD's are regularly scheduled meetings. Regardless, however, of whether it is the annual ARD, the 3-year evaluation, a failure
ARD, or an ARD called by the parent, these meetings commonly
follow a planned agenda. This agenda includes the following:

1. Introduction of all participants attending the meeting
2. Reading of the minutes
3. Announcement of the purpose of the meeting
4. Review of assessment data
5. Review of the IEP (Individual Educational Plan)
6. Development of appropriate modifications for the IEP or
   development of the IEP for the next school year
7. Establishing of proper national and/or state testing settings
8. Signature of the proper forms

An ARD meeting must have a designated person to take notes and fill out the proper forms. The administrator is responsible for following the ARD agenda and for assigning a recorder. Sometimes ARD meetings are taped for an accurate record of the information discussed.

Preparation for ARD meetings consists of gathering information about the student from diagnostic testing, the parent(s), the classroom teacher, and other involved professionals.

Union Grievance Meetings

Union grievance meetings, which are called to arbitrate employees' allegations of unfair or unequal treatment in the application of established policies, are another example of planned meetings. Those in attendance will include the individual(s) who brought the grievance, his or her immediate superior and/or the district superintendent, and—depending on the nature and gravity of the allegation—attorneys representing the parties, union representatives, and/or professional arbitrators. Because some of the people involved may be under stress, it is especially important to carefully follow protocol during a grievance meeting, to ensure that the hearing is fair and that the meeting proceeds smoothly.

Preparation for a grievance meeting involves gathering written documents pertaining to the grievance, including relevant policies, rules and regulations, and/or any written documentation that has been generated. Leaders should prepare for union grievance meetings by learning as much as possible about the nature of and the parties to the grievance and by anticipating the types of questions that will be asked.

Community Meetings

Community meetings fall into two categories: those that are planned for you and those you plan. Community meetings that are planned for you usually offer an opportunity for you to speak to an audience for a brief period of time. Keep in mind that your presentation usually takes place following dinner and after the club business is completed. Keep it short and sweet and be prepared for a number of questions. As a general rule, try to speak about an aspect of education that you are familiar with, making three to five points. Then recap and close with a request for questions from the audience. It's fine to use note cards containing key phrases or quotes, but you should avoid reading directly from your prepared speech or notes. The best approach, if you have time, is to first research the literature on the subject, developing an outline and visual aids, and then to practice your prepared speech so that it appears that you are speaking directly *to* your audience, not *at* your audience.

Community meetings you plan generally involve participation among various individuals and organizations, including parents, business leaders, and representatives from community support groups, who strive for a common educational goal. This type of meeting can be difficult to organize because of the potential for conflicting schedules. It is best to appoint a steering committee and establish meeting dates several weeks ahead of time so that they may be placed on business calendars. Reminders in the form of mail-outs and phone calls also encourage participation. Some helpful hints for organizing community meetings include the following:

1. Learn the names of business secretaries, and develop an ongoing rapport with these individuals.
2. Mail agendas at least 2 weeks in advance, followed by postcard and phone call reminders.
3. Give everyone in the meeting an important responsibility or goal to accomplish.
4. Keep in mind that some players cannot attend every meeting. Don't become discouraged if someone can't attend at the last minute.
5. Follow up every meeting with written minutes and distribute to all players whether or not they attended. End written minutes with the time and date of the next meeting.

Opening and Closing School Meetings

The last type of planned meetings that occur during the course of the school year include the opening and closing school meetings.

These, of course, have their own separate agendas and courses of action, and all faculty and support personnel are required to attend them.

The opening school meeting is the time when the school mission is discussed, the goals of the school year are outlined, and any changes in the state mandates are reviewed.

The closing school meetings sometimes consist only of a packet of information on check-out procedures, but this meeting is also a time to reflect on those goals established at the beginning of the school year and to assess the progress made toward meeting those goals. Closure on the past year's goals will help facilitate the creation of the next year's goals. Tentative goals for the upcoming school year should be outlined, and proposed changes in curriculum, procedures, and budget should be discussed.

Unplanned Meetings

Planned meetings, where you have the opportunity to create, mold and refine the purpose of gathering, can be rewarding. On the other hand, unplanned meetings—simply because they are unexpected—can seem dangerous and stressful. They are more difficult to prepare for because they always seem to occur when we have little time to deal with the situation, and they must always be dealt with immediately and accurately. The best defense for the unplanned meeting is to plan ahead for these types of meetings by developing rules, policies, and plans of action. Unplanned meetings include some parent conferences, student discipline, media events, and crisis situations.

Parent Conferences

Some parent meetings may be unplanned. When the parent storms into the office without calling ahead to schedule an appointment with you, that's an unplanned parent conference.

Keep in mind that upset parents believe there is good reason to be upset and that, in many cases, it may have nothing to do with you personally. In any case, always let the parent talk first. Do not interrupt or try to reason immediately. Above all, remain calm. Once you lose control, you lose respect. With lost respect, rumors run wild. Always remember parents can talk about you, but because of your position you are not free to talk about parents. But you may be sure that if you lose control, it will be discussed in the grocery store line and at work, and will soon be all over town!

Experience has taught us to let the parent get everything "off his chest" first. A good way to do this is to ask the parent to make a list of what is troubling him or her. List-making helps the parent to focus on the immediate problem and defuses some of the anger and potential for personal attacks on the "system" or faculty member(s). Once the parent has listed all the items that have led to the meeting, you can then address each item separately.

The following are useful tips for handling unplanned parent meetings:

1. Remember that the other person is upset, not you. *Keep it that way.*
2. Escort the person into a quiet private room.
3. Let the person talk freely. Do not interrupt.
4. Listen intently.
5. Show your concern.
6. Acknowledge his or her feelings.
7. Restate his or her concerns.
8. Ask if there is anything else; ask again if necessary.
9. Ask for clarification if you don't understand.
10. Search for and find common ground.
11. Once common ground is found, build together.

For those unplanned parent phone call meetings, tape this list next to your phone so that you can be sure to keep your cool!

Another useful technique for handling unplanned parent meetings is to take notes and ask questions about their concerns. Show surprise. Ask them how they would handle it if they were in your shoes and what they think it will take to solve the problem. If you feel unprepared or unable to resolve the situation quickly and satisfactorily, ask for time to gather information and offer to get back with them in a few days. Call back after investigating the situation and report your findings. If matters still remain unsettled, arrange for another conference. The passage of time will tend to cool everyone off and increase the probability of reaching a swift, painless resolution.

Student Discipline

Many student discipline problems can also be classified as unplanned meetings because, like unplanned parent conferences, they aren't easily predicted and require immediate attention. The types of student conduct that may result in disciplinary action can vary, depending on the established state and local school board policies. Generally speaking, disciplinary action is taken for behaviors such as fighting; possession of weapons, illegal drugs, alcohol, or tobacco on campus; gang-related activities, as established by state or local policy; violation of the school's student code of conduct; and other inappropriate behaviors, such as sexual harassment, that interfere with the education of students.

Sometimes inappropriate behavior can be handled most effectively by the adult who observes or is notified about the infraction. In more serious instances, it may be necessary to bring in an administrator, the students' parents, or law enforcement members.

The best advance strategy for handling student discipline problems is to develop, implement, and distribute a discipline management plan at the beginning of the school year for all students. A good discipline management plan will follow state mandates and local school board policies in defining what are acceptable and unacceptable student behaviors. Establish a fair student code of conduct and request that all faculty members turn in their individual classroom rules. Once clear procedures and expectations for behavior are established, student discipline problems can be quickly resolved and thus will be less disruptive to classroom procedures.

Media Events

Media events are generally unplanned, as are the meetings that ensue between educators and members of the press. Most often, they involve a request from a newspaper, radio, or television reporter for your point of view on some controversial issue within education that affects your school or your professional situation. Again, the best way to handle media meetings is to be prepared. Keeping up-to-date with current events and practicing interview techniques will increase both your effectiveness and your credibility as an education spokeperson. Helpful interview techniques include the following:

1. Keep current with issues affecting education in your community.
2. Have someone videotape your answers to "tough" questions.
3. Be honest and sincere in your responses.
4. Don't talk "for the record" about something you are unsure of.
5. Answer only the questions asked; don't volunteer any more information than is necessary.

Crisis Situations

The last type of unplanned meeting occurs when there is a crisis, either within the school community or in the community-at-large. Crisis situations may stem from natural disasters, such as tornados, hurricanes, blizzards, severe thunderstorms, dust storms, earthquakes, floods, and fires. They also may include human disasters, such as toxic spills; campus shootings, kidnappings, or hostage-taking; the death of a student, teacher, or a community or political leader; gang-related incidents; student walk-outs; and union strikes.

It is important to have a clear plan of action in place before a crisis occurs. The two primary elements to consider when designing a crisis plan of action are (1) assigning and defining the specific duties of key personnel and (2) ensuring the safety of employees and students.

Key personnel are those people who have been authorized and are responsible for contacting the police department, fire department, hospital, and physicians in the event of an emergency. The school should have at least two key people for every 50 students who will know who to contact and how to proceed in a crisis situation.

Natural-disaster planning includes both establishing evacuation plans and regularly practicing the procedures throughout the year. Develop safety procedures to use during human-generated crises and discuss these strategies during faculty meetings. Knowing ahead of time who to contact and what specific steps to take helps everyone to stay calm and keep order when a disaster actually occurs.

Meetings come in all shapes and sizes, have diverse goals and participants, and can range from spur-of-the-moment encounters to formal and highly-organized conferences, but they all share the same basic characteristics. Each is composed of a program, participants, production, and—to the greatest practical extent—preparation.

In addition, for meetings that can be planned, one more element is required: a planner, someone who will take responsibility for ensuring that everything is in place and that, once started, the meeting runs smoothly.

The degree of one's skill at planning and conducting "user-friendly" meetings can make or break a professional career. Fortunately, it is not an inborn trait, but a craft that can be learned. The next chapter outlines what you need to know and do to guarantee that the next meeting you organize is a success.

3

How to Plan Successful Meetings

R emember when you began teaching just a few years ago? That first job was filled with excitement, anticipation, and a little bit of fear. You wondered constantly if the students would like you, if you were really ready for this job, and if you could ever get your classroom as organized and as nicely decorated as Mrs. Johnson's down the hall in Room 24.

Mrs. Johnson's room was one that stimulated learning. She came in 2 weeks before the first day of school to prepare her classroom for the students. Posters were carefully hung in just the right spots. Bookshelves were full of neatly stacked books and the desks were clean and arranged just so. Sun-catchers and live plants decorated the windows.

Mrs. Johnson's desk was clean and organized. Every book she planned to use during the school year was neatly aligned in the left-hand corner of her desk between two apple book stands. An apple pencil holder contained six freshly sharpened pencils, and a three-inch stack of papers occupied the right-hand corner.

When the first day of school arrived, Mrs. Johnson stood outside her classroom door greeting each student with a smile and a twinkling eye. The students entered the room and found their names already on their new desks. On the board in large letters was written,

"Welcome to Chemistry I. I am glad you are here!" Remember when?

Mrs. Johnson was well-organized. She had completed all the backstage chores, and the stage was set for her first meeting with her new students. Mrs. Johnson would run this meeting smoothly because she knew the type of stage necessary and because all the preparations needed to accomplish it had been anticipated and handled ahead of time.

A successful meeting is like Mrs. Johnson's classroom. All of the elements to establish stimulating meetings must be anticipated and handled ahead of time. The stage must be set for learning, exchanging ideas, and communicating thoughts. For success time after time, plan your meeting as Mrs. Johnson planned her class.

Determining if a Meeting Is Necessary

Call meetings only when absolutely necessary; that is, when the item(s) of business cannot be taken care of in a one- or two-page memo, when you have three or more items that require immediate input from your employees (see Resource B: Meeting in the Mailbox), or when one or more of the following questions cannot be answered immediately:

1. *What* needs to be done?
2. *How* can it be accomplished?
3. *When* is the right time to do it? (See Resource C: Pre-Meeting Planner)

Purpose of the Meeting

Once you have determined a meeting is necessary and once you have a list of the items of business, you'll find the purpose for the meeting has already been established—that is, the purpose is to address the listed items and to gather input on the three critical questions. The discussion topics can come from a variety of sources. In schools, new mandates and/or laws generally trigger the need for a meeting, but students, teachers, custodians, and even parents may generate the ideas or concerns to be addressed.

In inviting people to the meeting, state the purpose clearly in one or two sentences and/or key words or phrases. Doing so allows others the opportunity to think about the meeting and their experiences in relation to the purpose, in advance. If you cannot write a clear purpose statement, don't schedule a meeting—even if it's one typically held every Wednesday. A simple announcement that "no meeting is necessary this week" will gain you credibility.

Determining Who Comes

Once the purpose for the meeting is established, the leader should determine who needs to attend. Because all participants should be directly involved in the "what" and "how" and "when" questions, decide whether the entire faculty or only representatives within the faculty should be invited. If all faculty members need to hear the same information, then all faculty members need to attend. If the meeting can be successfully accomplished with representatives, then schedule only those individuals. No one likes to attend a meeting not directly relevant to them (see Resource D: Who-to-Invite Checklist).

Communicating the Agenda

The agenda for a meeting can be a very powerful tool in making your meetings highly effective ones. If done right, it communicates the urgency and importance of the meeting. Agenda items typically are brief statements that directly relate to the purpose of the meeting. Individuals want to know exactly why the meeting is needed and what part they will play. Agenda items listed as "budget development" do very little to speed up or clarify the underlying issue of budget reduction. A much more powerful strategy is to use the question format, such as, "How do you think we can cut our proposed budget by 10%?" or "How can we save our duplicating costs by 5% this next year?" Agenda items help "set the stage" to focus on the issues at hand. Use the ABC's (accuracy, brevity, and clarity) of writing to prepare the agenda (see Resource E: Sample Team Agenda).

Handouts

Once the agenda is set, consider whether handouts are needed. Handouts can be used to (1) provide background information; (2) summarize important concepts to be discussed; (3) check for understanding; and/or (4) provide follow-up activities. Generally speaking, you will need one copy per person, plus 10%. Nothing is more frustrating for participants than not getting a handout because the leader miscalculated.

Handouts should be carefully selected. Most people do not have time to read several pages of documents. As the leader of the meeting, choose one, maybe two, key articles or charts that best supplement the agenda topic(s). Meeting participants appreciate leaders who keep handouts to a minimum.

Establishing Time and Site

Once the agenda for the meeting has been decided and handouts have been selected, check the school calendar to determine the best possible date and time for all participants. When appropriate, check the community calendar also. Unfortunately, it is not always possible to set meeting times that will fit everyone's schedules; however, the more notice people are given of the meeting time and date, the greater is the likelihood that they will either be available or can rearrange their schedules to accommodate the meeting.

Meeting site is important. We have all attended meetings that were poorly planned—meetings that were standing room only or ones held in classrooms neatly lined up in rows with the leader behind the infamous teacher's desk. The site, just like Mrs. Johnson preparing for her students the first day of class, should be carefully arranged. If the meeting is a brainstorming session or idea exchange, the room should be arranged so that no one is "leading." Tables work great; however, they do not accommodate large groups. In instances when you need to communicate with a large number of people, but when you also want feedback, consider scheduling a series of smaller, less informal meetings. Or meet together as a large group, then break down into smaller groups, then reconvene in the large group setting. This method allows everyone an opportunity to speak within the smaller group, so that each person can feel involved in the meeting process.

Recruiting Someone to Take Minutes

It is important to have someone take minutes of the meeting in order to record information that is necessary to reach a decision, come to consensus, and/or to plan. Three key questions should guide the writing of minutes:

1. What was discussed?
2. Who said what?
3. Consensus and/or decision?

Because it is almost impossible to record every word spoken, focus on the major information. In faculty meetings where the agenda has been distributed as part of the invitation to participate, leave plenty of space between agenda items so that participants may record their own personal notes. When the minutes of the meeting are then typed, the headings are associated with the invitational meeting agenda. For example:

You are invited to attend the faculty meeting scheduled for Thursday, May 25, from 3:40 p.m. to 4:30 p.m. in the high school library. The purpose of this meeting is to discuss the following items:

1. Need to decrease 1994-95 budget by 10%
2. Discipline Management Plan (DMP)
   a. What rules would you like to see established for ALL students?

b. How has our DMP worked for you?

c. What areas of the DMP do we need to improve to facilitate learning?

3. Cooperative Learning

a. What strategies worked successfully for you?

b. What strategies would you like to learn more about?

We have asked for volunteers, assigned people to record minutes, and have taken minutes ourselves. Minute-taking is most successful when one person, say the school secretary, is responsible for the minutes at all large faculty meetings. During smaller departmental meetings, assign one person as the recorder and rotate this responsibility so that everyone has an opportunity to take the minutes. We recommend establishing the procedure for recording minutes ahead of time, including designating the person responsible. Because the last item of business is usually setting the next meeting date, it is natural to also designate the recorder. This procedure helps communicate who is responsible for what (see Appendix F: Minutes of the SBM Meeting).

"It's the Little Things"

Our experience is that when meetings number five or more people, it's good to serve refreshments. This is not a precise rule or law, but people are always pleasantly surprised if there's something to eat or drink; it allows people a minute of time to relax and prepare for the planned agenda. Just make sure all necessary supplies are on hand: coffee ready, drinks cold, cups and napkins in place, and, most importantly, the trash can in full sight. Serving refreshments takes a little more time and effort on your part; however, it helps make individuals attending the meeting feel special.

Another "little thing": Have you ever attended a meeting when the light of the overhead projector blew? The leader almost always says, "It worked just a minute ago!" Yes, we are sure it did, but this little mishap wastes precious time. We have found it wise, when using any audiovisual equipment, to have a spare bulb, movie projector, or VCR handy or available within three minutes. Unfortunately, because this is not always possible, be prepared to punt with some other type of activity. Always prepare for the worst and have proper backups.

All these backstage chores are time consuming, tedious, and sometimes a downright pain; however, they can make or break a meeting. Effective leaders plan, like Mrs. Johnson, for every participant. Remember, a meeting is a leader's classroom.

Opening and Closing
Meetings Effectively

The leader's role in opening and closing meetings is crucial because participants are uncertain what to expect from the meeting unless the purpose is clarified at the outset. It is equally important that the leader summarize afterward what was accomplished during the meeting. In other words, the leader's role is to ensure that people see and understand what is happening. Covey, in *The 7 Habits of Highly Effective People* (1992), emphasizes the need for leaders to pay attention to details, which include: getting to the meeting site early, establishing climate, facilitating the meeting, observing participant behavior, building consensus, closing the meeting, evaluating the meeting, and acting on evaluations.

Getting There Early

Getting to the meeting site early gives you the opportunity to ensure that everything is ready. Always arrive a few minutes before the meeting to see that the temperature is appropriate, seating is arranged, refreshments are in place, and handouts, (pertinent articles, meeting evaluations, and extra agendas) are distributed. These few minutes can be used to check the physical preparations and to psychologically prepare yourself for the meeting (Dyer & Williams, 1988).

Establishing Climate

Establishing the climate is the second responsibility for opening and closing the meeting. Create a positive, friendly climate by making eye contact and greeting each person by name when he or she enters the room. Also, start the meeting on time. Nothing is more frustrating for those who arrive on time than being told, "We will wait a few minutes for so-and-so." Of equal importance to starting on time is ending on time. When people are informed that the meeting will end at a certain time and it doesn't, they understandably get upset. We should have the same commitment to starting and ending a meeting on time as we do to starting and ending a class on time.

Facilitating the Meeting

Facilitating the meeting is the third task under opening and closing the meeting. Some researchers think the group leader should chair all meetings (Whitehead, 1983); others believe that chairing should be rotated among all participants. Regardless of who chairs, it is imperative that there be someone designated to facilitate the meeting. Facilitating involves carefully observing as well as listening to people. According to Covey (1992), 10% of human communication is through words; 30% is through sounds, and 60% is through body language. Clearly, the chairperson must be tuned-in to body language meaning, if there is to be open communication and full participation by all members. For example, when members engage in side conversations, the grading of papers, or letter-writing, this may signal that they are bored or that they feel the topic is irrelevant. Appropriate responses to off-task behaviors are to ask those individuals if they have questions or to simply stare at them until they refocus. An individual who sends out a closed-body-language message, such as crossed arms and tucked legs, may be angry or defensive.

Another kind of body language to carefully observe is eye contact. During normal conversation, frequent eye contact is maintained. When someone looks away for a sustained period of time, it normally suggests rejection. Avoiding eye contact altogether can indicate insecurity or a wish to be elsewhere, whereas staring implies hostility. Remember that nonverbal language communicates what people are really feeling. All negative messages, whether they are verbal or nonverbal, should be dealt with openly and settled to everyone's satisfaction before moving on to the next item of business. Conflicts left unattended and unresolved can sabotage the group and make meaningful teamwork—and progress—impossible. (See chapter 5 for more on conflict management.)

Observing Participant Behavior

A fourth leader task tied in closely to facilitation is observing participant behavior. People's responses and levels of participation in meetings may vary because they have diverse personality characteristics. People tend to be either extroverted (outspoken, relaxed, and spontaneous) or introverted (reflective and observant, rather than participatory). Ask the extrovert to chair subcommittees and take a more active role. On the other hand, ask the introvert to provide insight on various agenda items.

Besides these basic personality differences, people also differ in how they best perceive and process information. A "senser" wants an agenda, deals with facts, and relies on experience. An "intuiter" is interested in exploring possibilities, is future-oriented, and sees the "big picture." It is important to have both sensers and intuiters involved in the problem-solving process.

Individuals vary not only in personality and information-processing skills, but also in being primarily "thinkers" or "feelers." Thinkers are task-oriented and skeptical. They need to feel competent and are partial to facts. Feelers consider what is right and wrong, show emotion, seek consensus, and focus on people. Thinkers move the discussion along by debating the practical pros and cons of an issue. Feelers concentrate on the values related to an issue. Again, both approaches are necessary for effective problem solving during meetings.

Finally, there are differences in the ways people establish priorities. "Perceivers" want to gather as much information as possible prior to making a decision. "Judgers" want to act quickly so they can keep things moving. As personality types, both perceivers and judgers contribute valuable input to effective meetings.

Building Consensus

Consensus building was discussed in chapter 1 and is briefly mentioned here to emphasize its importance. It is stressed because even though consensus is difficult to reach, it means that people will "buy into" what is going to happen. After reaching consensus, review how implementation is going. Never assume consensus is the last step; implementation and subsequent follow-up are "musts."

Closing and Evaluating the Meeting

This step is just as crucial as opening the meeting. In closing, review major discussion items, decisions, pertinent timeliness, and items that need to be carried over to the next meeting. Also remind participants to complete and return meeting evaluation forms. A quick and easy evaluation format is the "Blip," which is simply a sheet stating, "To me, the meeting. . . . " In this way, participants state any positives or negatives they wish to address (see Resource G). Obviously, the "Blip" avoids asking for a signature or anything that would identify the person completing the evaluation, thereby ensuring anonymity (Shelton, 1989).

Acting on Evaluations

The final component of effective meetings entails following up on participant evaluations. Evaluations are used to improve meetings, just as student evaluations are used to improve teaching. Never hold evaluations against staff members. At the next meeting, briefly comment on the fact that some good suggestions were made for improving meetings and that those suggestions will be followed up on. If suggestions are not heeded, then don't ask people to complete evaluations. Why be a hypocrite? (see Resources H, I, J, K, and L).

In sum, opening and closing the meeting entails more than meets the eye. Make sure the environment is right; value participants for their uniqueness; make decisions on a consensus basis; highlight key points from the meeting; and act on evaluations. In other words, make sure that participants see and understand what is going on and what has gone on.

Managing Conflict in Meetings

Although some degree of organizational conflict is inevitable, conflict itself is neither innately good nor bad. Organizations with little or no conflict grow stagnant; too much conflict within organizations destroys staff morale and fosters high staff turnover. Conflict often arises during meetings, and a good leader must be ready to manage it. This chapter suggests ways to practice effective communication skills, identify your personal conflict management style, set ground rules for conflict, work through the conflict process, and use individual maturity levels—all of which help to keep conflict at a manageable level.

Effective Communication Skills

Basic to conflict management is practicing good communication skills. Three such skills relate to listening: disarming, empathy, and inquiry.

The first listening skill, *disarming*, is the most difficult, but it is also the most powerful: You simply listen and then find something to agree with in what the other person is saying. This can defuse a potentially volatile situation. For example, in a faculty meeting Maggie says, "This new teacher duty schedule you created is a mess; more people are on duty than we need. We just end up standing there looking at one another. There's nothing to do. It's a total waste of time." You disarm her by saying, "Maggie, you're right. The duty schedule does need work. I need to know why it is not working and how we might improve it. What do you recommend we do to make it better?" With this response, you have identified, acknowledged, and restated her concerns and, by indicating your willingness to listen, you have opened the door for dialogue instead of argument.

The second listening skill, *empathy*, requires that you put yourself in the other person's shoes and look at the world through his or her eyes, either by paraphrasing what the individual says or by identifying with his or her feelings. An example: During a curriculum meeting, Marie, a veteran teacher, angrily says, "All of this curriculum revision you are making us do is ridiculous. We go through this every time we get a new principal, and quite honestly, you won't last long enough to see any of it finished." This is a frontal assault that, if taken personally, can easily degenerate into a shouting match. An empathic response is to say, "O.K. This is what I hear you saying: that you spend all this time working on curriculum yet you feel nothing is ever accomplished by it. I would find that very frustrating, too. What do you suggest we do differently?" Not only have you restated Marie's concern about the curriculum revision, you have also shown some feeling for the frustration she is experiencing. Because most people respond positively to an empathic approach, there is an increased likelihood of working together to resolve the conflict.

The third listening skill, *inquiry*, allows you to ask gentle, probing questions to determine what is going on. After gathering additional insight, it's possible to work with the conflict. For example, Pete, a first-year teacher, says, "I'm so fed up that I am going to quit. There's no way I'm going to make it as a teacher. I can't control the kids; they just don't seem to care. I just don't have what it takes." In response, ask a question along these lines. "Pete, what is the matter? What is going on?" Your inquiry is genuine, yet opens the door for Pete to describe his feelings.

So far we've looked at three excellent skills: disarming, empathy, and inquiry. Now let's turn to self-expression skills, specifically "I" statements and stroking. Beginning statements with "I" is probably the easiest communication skill to use because your own feelings are centered and recognized, rather than placing the other person on the defensive. Instead of saying, "You make me so mad. You are so stupid and what you've done will probably get us into a lawsuit;" say, "I am angry, Fred, because of the manner in which this problem was handled. I'm afraid we'll end up in a lawsuit." By beginning with "I," you own the anger that helps Fred know exactly where you are emotionally. It also allows him to present his side of the story without feeling he is on the defensive.

In the self-expression skill of stroking, you find something positive to say about the other person, even in the heat of battle. By so doing, the incident is separated out from the person. Listen to this: "Jamie, there is no one I respect more than you as a teacher, but I am very concerned about the way in which the cheerleader tryouts were handled." What you have done is stroke Jamie for being a fine teacher, but you also have indicated your concern about one specific incident—cheerleader tryouts. With stroking, cheerleader tryouts are put into perspective and Jamie still knows he is respected for his teaching, even though the tryouts didn't go right.

Basically through using the foregoing techniques, others' thoughts and feelings are recognized. You model respect, even though you disagree or are upset with the person. Remember, only through practicing effective communication skills can conflict be managed; conflict doesn't simply disappear when it is ignored.

Determining Conflict Management Style

How do you manage conflict? Your personal conflict leadership style sets the parameters around which you work. One such leadership style is similar to that of a lawyer; everyone involved in the conflict gets something. Another style is that of policy analyst, where detailed data is analyzed to determine what will be done about the conflict. A more rigid style is that of financial analyst, which looks strictly at money (loss and profit). Still another is the style related to political science, which considers people's reactions. How will Joe respond if we do this? How will Betty take it? Along with examining people's reactions, you also take a look at the winners and losers. What will the teachers' union get out of this? Will the decision put the school board in a bad situation? Yet another style is that of efficiency expert, who makes decisions based on the effects they will have on the school mission and objectives.

In other situations, an organizational behaviorialist style may be best, in order to encourage people to be open and honest. In the behavioralist mode, people are even encouraged to disagree with you, the boss. In this scenario, emphasis is on people and satisfying their concerns. Still another approach is that of the "professional expert"; that is, simply controlling and dominating others. Because you have all the answers, just tell people what to do; their input isn't needed. The final style involves relying on the secretary; the lens through which your secretary perceives conflict becomes your filter for managing conflict. The secretarial leadership style is very prevalent in organizations, even though most leaders openly disclaim it.

Different leadership styles are appropriate in different conflict situations; just remember to be fair, respectful, and confidential.

Setting Ground Rules

After determining your conflict management style, set ground rules for conflict using nontechnical language. People need to know what is and is not acceptable. Generally speaking, encourage lively, open debate; identify common problems; avoid winner-take-all solutions; wipe out the historical slate; include affected people; and ensure everyone gets the same information. It sounds simple enough, but it's shocking how often these rules are thrown out when personalities take the forefront and hostility increases.

Processing Conflict

Succinctly stated, conflict management is a process that begins with understanding staff members' styles, agendas, and quirks. People have "baggage" from past experiences, which shape their present perceptions and behaviors. When someone is stuck on the garbage and is unable to progress, it's helpful to go one-on-one and discuss past and present perceptions. However, after listening, bring the individual up to the present. Encourage the person to move toward a positive attitude and to keep the larger organizational goals in mind.

The most critical part of the conflict management process is reaching agreement. The process allows everyone to say what's on his or her mind, but personalities must be left out. As people speak, you as the leader synthesize what is being said. Encourage the people with closed body language, anger, disagreement, or boredom to speak up. It's imperative for them to express their feelings. Once the cards are out on the table and everyone has the chance to voice concerns, then it is possible to brainstorm solutions.

After the brainstorming session, work toward consensus on one or several solutions. Conflict resolution is much easier when everyone buys into a decision or reaches consensus on the course of action. After consensus, repeat points of agreement and describe what will take place in the future. After implementing solutions, check with concerned parties and determine how things are going and what remains to be done.

Using Maturity Levels

During the conflict management process, it's also helpful to consider people's maturity levels in relation to the organization. The more mature they are, the less directive you need to be in managing conflict. And the reverse is also true. For individuals who are organizationally immature, use a very directive approach in managing conflict. These people generally don't want to be involved in conflict resolution because they are into survival and survival only. People who are a bit more organizationally mature desire greater input into conflict resolution, so carefully explain benefits of a given solution to them.

Those who have a still higher maturity level should be actively engaged in conflict resolution. Individuals who possess the highest maturity level of any staff members should resolve conflict themselves. In other words, delegate conflict resolution to them. They can solve their own problems.

When considering employee maturity levels, be sure you're assessing individuals accurately. It's far better to assume a person is at a higher than lower maturity level, rather than to insult the individual.

In sum, good conflict management means being open, honest, and straightforward. When you are upset with someone, talk to that person one-on-one. Hit conflict head-on. It's far better to confront conflict than to let it grow and escalate. Conflict is healthy, as long as it is depersonalized. Deal with the issue, not the personality. Remember that conflict surfaces when change occurs, so don't try to squelch it; work through the process. Schools benefit when people thoroughly discuss and even disagree on teaching and learning. Remember that you are modeling and shaping culture by demonstrating that conflict—and conflict resolution—are both natural and positive.

Conclusion

In *Secrets of Highly Effective Meetings*, we have emphasized how important meetings are in fostering culture, communication, morale and problem solving. Meetings occur for reasons that range from formal disciplinary proceedings to spur-of-the-moment, impromptu conferences to crisis responses. Whatever the purpose, the first secret of any successful meeting is planning—where possible—and preparation. For most meetings for which there is advance notice, follow these steps:

- Determine if a meeting is necessary. Do not call a meeting if the business can be accomplished another way.
- Establish the purpose(s) of the meeting.
- Decide who should attend.
- Gather input for and distribute the agenda.
- Develop and distribute handouts at the beginning of the meeting.
- Set the meeting's time and site.
- Recruit someone to take minutes.
- Serve refreshments.

The second secret of effective meetings is to make sure they are properly opened and closed. Keep the following points in mind:

- Arrive at the meeting site early to ensure that everything is set up and ready.
- Establish a warm, caring environment.
- Facilitate the meeting through observation, careful listening, and consensus building.
- At the end of the meeting, restate what has been agreed to.
- Evaluate the meeting.
- Act on the evaluations.

The final secret of highly effective meetings is to manage and resolve the conflict that occurs during the course of meetings. Use the following conflict management strategies:

- Disarm by listening to and finding something to agree with in what the other person is saying.
- Empathize by placing yourself in the other person's shoes and imagining what he or she is feeling.
- Inquire by asking gentle, probing questions that begin with "I."
- Lead by being fair, respectful, and confidential.
- Set ground rules by stating what are acceptable and what are unacceptable behaviors.
- Process conflict by understanding a person's past "baggage" and bringing him or her up to the present.
- Hit conflict head-on by dealing with it directly.

Follow our guidelines and we're sure that your next meeting—and all those that come after—will be both more productive *and* a good reflection on you. Then do your fellow meeting-goers a favor, and share *Secrets of Highly Effective Meetings* with a friend.

Resources

Resource A

TO: MEMBERS OF THE SBM* TEAM
FROM: LAURIE BAUER
DATE:

SUBJECT: INVITATION TO ATTEND THE SBM MEETING (DATE)

Dear SBM Team Members,

You are invited to attend the SBM meeting on (date) at 7:30 a.m. in Room 212. The purpose of this meeting is to discuss the following items:

1. Reading and writing across the curriculum

2. Senate Bill 7

3. Other concerns/problems

* Site-Based Management

Resource B

TO: FACULTY MEMBERS
FROM: LAURIE BAUER
DATE:

SUBJECT: MEETING IN THE MAILBOX

Dear Faculty Members,

I would like to commend all of you for your hard work and dedication during the first week of school. The first 3 days went smoothly and I thank you for your cooperation in moving into and opening a new school and adjusting to the new environment. We still have a few problems with lockers; however, we hope to be able to solve that this week. Sam Jones says that the "reconstruction" is right on schedule and indicates he will be finished within 2 weeks. (Keep your fingers crossed!)

There are some concerns I would like to clarify that include the following:

1. Hall passes
2. Tear strips
3. Clocks
4. Textbooks NOT passed out to students
5. Special education monitor documents
6. Special education testing information

Hall Passes

Randall Martin suggested that we develop a standardized hall pass for students. Thank you, Randall! I will supply each teacher with his or her own hall pass, which can be reused. Until you receive your official passes, please use a piece of paper when allowing students in the hall during class time.

Tear Strips

Thank you all for turning in your tear strips so promptly. I have turned in a work order to have clips attached to the outside of each classroom door. Until they arrive and are installed, please continue to bring you tear strips to the office after your last scheduled class.

Second-period tear strips are our official documentation for state-funding purposes. Please follow these guidelines when completing the second-period tear strip:

1. Write your FULL NAME (just as if you were signing a check). Example: L. Bauer is WRONG! Laurie K. Bauer is CORRECT.
2. On the other slips (every period except second), you may abbreviate your name.
3. If a student is leaving your class for another (schedule change), draw a line through the ID# and initial the line. At the bottom of the slip, briefly explain the reason for the change. ANYTIME you make a mistake on the second-period slip, just draw a single line through the ID#, initial the line, and explain the error at the bottom. DO NOT MARK ANYONE "T" ON THE SECOND-PERIOD SLIP!
4. If a student is new to your class, print or write in the name and the ID# if you know it.
5. The full date must be written. Example: "8/25" is WRONG. "8/25/94" is CORRECT.

Tear strips this week DO NOT INCLUDE SCHEDULE CHANGES. Please add or remove names as indicated above. All schedule changes as of (date) have been completed, and Amy is presently adding them to the computer.

Clocks

I have placed clocks and AA batteries in your mailbox. If you have a clock in your classroom, please return the clock to the office so that it may be used elsewhere in the building.

Textbooks

It was suggested in the Site-Based Management (SBM) meeting that we cover classroom textbooks with brightly colored paper so that it would be more difficult for students to leave class with the textbook. I have purchased a neon pink paper to cover the textbooks you will be keeping in your classroom. Please come see Ms. Mc Cracken or myself to get this paper. I am warning you that it is BRIGHT!

Special Education Monitor Documents

Debbie Dodson will be giving each teacher the special education monitor documents. They will be placed in your mailbox either Friday evening or Monday morning.

Special Education Testing Information

There has been concern pertaining to handing tests in on Fridays. The purpose of turning in tests early is to help students isolate important information that they will be responsible for knowing. Students with learning disabilities tend to consider all information as equally important and have difficulty determining which information is most important to remember. To clarify:

1. Tests may be handed in on Fridays; however, if you cannot get the actual test in, then the following should be handed in:
   a. Outline of information (topics) you anticipate will be covered on the test
   b. Format of test and approximate number of questions; that is, 10 to 20 multiple-choice, 10 true and false, 20 matching, 3 to 5 short answer, and 1 to 2 essay
2. On the day the students are to be tested, turn in the test and modified test to Debbie Dodson.

If you have any other questions or concerns, please let me know.

Resource C

Should We Meet?

1. Can a memo be used instead of holding a meeting?
2. Is there a goal for the meeting?

Who Should Attend the Meeting?

3. Who needs to come to the meeting?
4. Will there be less than 15 participants?

The Setting

5. Where will the meeting be held?
6. Is the site convenient to participants?
7. Will a circular table arrangement be used?
8. Is the room temperature comfortable?
9. Have refreshments been arranged?

The Agenda

10. Have all participants been asked for agenda input?
11. Are the "For Information" items stated in sentence format?
12. Are the "For Discussion" items stated in question format?
13. Has the draft agenda been proofed?
14. Has the agenda been distributed, with at least 2 days lead time?

The Preparation

15. Have possible "troublesome items" been thought through?
16. If problem solving is a goal of the meeting, has the problem been adequately explained to meeting participants?
17. Has someone been asked to take minutes?
18. Has a follow-up on the previous evaluations been done?
19. Have evaluation forms (Blips) been distributed?

Resource D

After preparing the agenda, the next question is who to invite. The following checklist will help you determine the people to invite. Mark this sheet with checks in the categories to which the agenda items apply.

	Teachers	Support	Counselor	Parents
Agenda Item 1	———	———	———	———
Agenda Item 2	———	———	———	———
Agenda Item 3	———	———	———	———
Agenda Item 4	———	———	———	———
Is one representative from this group sufficient?	———	———	———	———

If the answer to the last question is YES, choose the representative. If the answer is NO, decide how many and who will be invited to attend.

Resource E

For Information

1. School dismisses January 6 at 2:00 p.m. The in-service for teachers begins at 2:30 p.m., in Room 200. Please bring your peer coaching materials. Refreshments provided.
2. The State Board of Education is offering 20 scholarships for teachers who wish to pursue their Gifted and Talented certification. Contact Joe Smith, secretary, for necessary paperwork.

3. "Hats off" to Mary Hernandez on receiving her master's degree in early childhood education from Texas A&M University. Also a big "hats off" to Herman Brown, custodian, on receiving his GED. Both of these people will be honored with a cake and refreshments in the Teacher's Lounge. A special mention will be made on Monday morning announcements for Mary's and Herman's accomplishments.

4. Yeah! Yeah! David Rogers, chemistry teacher, was awarded a 3-week scholarship to attend NASA's Science Teacher Institute in Huntsville, Alabama.

5. We are very proud of our "team" here at Sunshine Magnet School. We work to help one another.

For Discussion

1. What are four good things that have happened in the last week here at school?

2. What are your suggestions for the audiovisual budget? What "big ticket" items are needed? Bottom line—how will each piece of equipment help us better teach our kids?

3. How might the teacher duty schedule be revised to enhance the protection of students and to alleviate unnecessary teacher time?

4. Let's talk. How is morale? What can we do to improve morale?

5. How is team teaching going in Social Studies? Who is involved? What is being done? What impact does it have on student learning? What are the downsides? What are the strengths? How might administration facilitate? Should other departments/grade levels look at trying team teaching?

6. What items need to be placed on next week's team agenda?

Resource F

MINUTES OF THE SBM MEETING (DATE)

Members attending: E. Husmann, D. Dodson, J. Smith, D. Koenig, L. Bauer

Members absent: D. Cecil, B. Olson, S. Smith

1. Reading and writing across the curriculum
   It was the consensus to have ideas printed for implementing reading across the curriculum. The writing stamp was well received by the team.
2. Senate Bill 7—Accountability report
   Due to time addressing concerns and problems, Senate Bill 7 was not discussed.
3. Concerns/problems
   Concern: Teacher tutorials—receiving only their listing
   Solution: Tutorial lists will be posted by the office.
   Concern: Passing period not long enough
   Solution: Lengthen the passing period to 4 minutes.

cc: All SBM team members, superintendent, district principals

Resource G

BLIP

To me, the meeting was ————————.

Strengths of the meeting included ————————.

Weaknesses of the meeting included ————————.

Resource H

Please circle the appropriate number to the right of each statement; Number 1 signifies strongly disagree, whereas Number 5 signifies strongly agree. After completing the checklist, please place it in the chairperson's mailbox. To ensure anonymity, do not write your name on this instrument.

	Strongly Disagree				*Strongly Agree*
The environment					
1. The chairperson was warm and caring	1	2	3	4	5
2. The chairperson greeted participants by name	1	2	3	4	5
3. Participants could easily see and communicate with each other	1	2	3	4	5
4. The site was convenient to participants	1	2	3	4	5
5. The room temperature was comfortable	1	2	3	4	5
6. The chairs were the appropriate size for participants	1	2	3	4	5
7. The meeting lasted less than 1 1/2 hours	1	2	3	4	5
The chairperson					
8. The chairperson listened carefully and facilitated communication	1	2	3	4	5
9. The chairperson encouraged each participant to join in discussion	1	2	3	4	5
10. The chairperson effectively used humor	1	2	3	4	5
11. The chairperson showed respect for each participant	1	2	3	4	5
12. The chairperson synthesized key decisions and moved the discussion along	1	2	3	4	5

Resource I

CHAIRPERSON'S CHECKLIST

Please circle the appropriate number to the right of each statement; Number 1 signifies strongly disagree, whereas Number 5 signifies strongly agree.

The environment

		Strongly Disagree				Strongly Agree
1.	I was warm and friendly	1	2	3	4	5
2.	I greeted each participant	1	2	3	4	5
3.	Participants could see and communicate which each other	1	2	3	4	5
4.	The site was convenient for participants	1	2	3	4	5
5.	Room temperature was comfortable	1	2	3	4	5
6.	The chairs were the appropriate size for participants	1	2	3	4	5
7.	The meeting lasted less than 1 1/2 hours	1	2	3	4	5

The chairperson

8.	I listened and paraphrased what was being said	1	2	3	4	5
9.	I encouraged participants to openly enter into discussion	1	2	3	4	5
10.	I showed respect for each participant	1	2	3	4	5

Resource J

LEADER EFFECTIVENESS RATING

Here's how to score the "leader effectiveness rating" quiz. Give yourself 10 points (+10) for an always answer. For a sometimes, give yourself 5 points (+5). Score a negative 10 points (–10) for a no. You pass if your score is over 70. Good luck!

1. Do I plan each meeting to the same extent that I expect teachers to plan their classes?
   Always: ____ Sometimes: ____ No: ____ Score: ____
2. Do I have a specific goal(s) for each meeting?
   Always: ____ Sometimes: ____ No: ____ Score: ____
3. Do I distribute an error-proof agenda to each participant at least 2 days before we meet?
   Always: ____ Sometimes: ____ No: ____ Score: ____
4. Do all staff persons know they have the opportunity to give input on agenda items?
   Always: ____ Sometimes: ____ No: ____ Score: ____
5. Do I invite/include the people who have the responsibilities/expertise related to the meeting goals?
   Always: ____ Sometimes: ____ No: ____ Score: ____
6. Do I encourage each participant to take part in the discussion?
   Always: ____ Sometimes: ____ No: ____ Score: ____
7. Do I play "devil's advocate" to spark greater thinking and discussion?
   Always: ____ Sometimes: ____ No: ____ Score: ____
8. Do I allow participants to disagree with me?
   Always: ____ Sometimes: ____ No: ____ Score: ____
9. Do I carefully observe and respond to participant body language?
   Always: ____ Sometimes: ____ No: ____ Score: ____
10. Do I make sure that no one person dominates discussion, including myself?
    Always: ____ Sometimes: ____ No: ____ Score: ____

    Total score: _____

Resource K

THE MEETING CHECKLIST

Please circle the appropriate number to the right of the statement; Number 1 signifies strongly disagree, whereas Number 5 signifies strongly agree. After completing the checklist, please place it in the chairperson's mailbox. To ensure anonymity, do not write your name on this instrument.

		Strongly Disagree			*Strongly Agree*	
1.	The meeting goal was clearly explained at the onset of the meeting	1	2	3	4	5
2.	The meeting goal warranted the meeting	1	2	3	4	5
3.	It was apparent that the meeting goal had been met when decisions, implementation, and timeliness were summarized	1	2	3	4	5

Resource L

THINGS I WANT TO REMEMBER FOR THE NEXT MEETING

1.

2.

3.

4.

5.

Annotated Bibliography
and References

Bolman, L., & Deal, T. (1984). *Modern approaches to understanding and managing organizations.* San Francisco: Jossey-Bass.

Among other topics, the authors present a bold, forthright approach to meetings. They point out that meetings are held for various reasons: making decisions, manipulating others, telling stories, sharing feelings, and keeping the organization going.

Covey, S. (1992). *The 7 habits of highly effective people.* New York: Simon & Schuster.

The author stresses that we see the world through a lens or paradigm, and that lens affects how we view the world. Effective people practice 7 habits for managing their lives: 1) proactively responding, 2) beginning with an end in mind, 3) putting first things first, 4) thinking win-win, 5) understanding and then being understood, 6) synergizing, and 7) self-renewing.

Deal, T., & Kennedy, A. (1982). *Corporate cultures: The rites and rituals of corporate life.* Reading, MA: Addison-Wesley.

The authors discuss organizational culture and its components: environment, values, heroes, rites and rituals, and network. They also emphasize that newcomers fail in organizations not because they lack technical skills but because they misread the culture.

Deal, T., & Peterson, K. (1990). *The principal's role in shaping school culture.* Washington, DC: Office of Educational Research and Improvement.

The authors emphasize that the principal's role in shaping school culture is just as important as that of instructional leader. The principal symbolizes the culture. Insofar as culture is concerned, the principal must "walk the talk."

De Bruyn, R. L., and Benjamin, J. M. (1983). *Mastering meetings.* Manhattan. KS: Master Teacher.

Dyer, D., & Williams, O. (1988). *Developing effective and efficient local committees.* Kellogg Foundation. (ERIC Document Reproduction Service No. 340 911)

The authors elaborate on the chairperson's role in setting meeting decorum and agenda. The use of problem solving in meetings is also discussed.

Frase, L., & Melton, R. (1992). Manager or participatory leader? What does it take? *NASSP Bulletin, 76,* 17-24.

Basic details of meetings are covered, such as meeting only when necessary; involving only the individuals who are affected; preparing an agenda; starting on time; and keeping minutes.

Gorton, R., & Burns, J. (1985). Faculty meetings: What do teachers really think of them? *The Clearing House, 59,* 30-32.

The authors discuss teachers' negative perceptions of faculty meetings. Even though meetings may not be as negative as teachers perceive them, "perception is reality," and chairpersons must work to correct misconceptions.

Lamon, S., & Shelton, M. (1991). We've got to stop meeting like this! *Principal, 71,* 54-55.

The authors humorously give ingredients for guaranteeing meeting failure. On the serious side, a sidebar highlights essential ingredients of effective meetings.

Leithwood, K., & Musella, D. (1991). *Understanding school system administration.* Falmer: New York.

The authors discuss how time is wasted in meetings. Specifics of several studies are given.

Mamchur, C. (1991). *How to run productive meetings.* Association for Curriculum and Supervision Development. (ERIC Document Reproduction Service No. 328 967)

The author details how different personality types (extrovert, introvert, sensor, intuiter, thinker, feeler, perceiver, and judger) impact one's preferences and behaviors. Suggestions are given for ways leaders can work with all personality types so that meetings will be effective.

Napier, R., & Gershenfeld, M. (1983). *Making groups work.* Boston: Houghton Mifflin.

The authors address why meeting participants get upset, such as they aren't being heard, new ideas are blocked, feelings are ignored, they are unable to get information, or they feel powerless to control the present situation.

Nigro, K. (1984). *Developing confidence and self-motivation in teachers: The role of the administrator.* Eastern New Mexico University. (ERIC Document Reproduction Service No. ED 269 842)

Novick, B. (1987). *Vocational educational administrators management training program phase III.* New Jersey State Department of Education. (ERIC Document Reproduction Service No. 227 249)

The author lists several components of successful meetings: stating the purpose of meeting, solving problems, recognizing task and maintenance functions, and enhancing creativity.

Schein, E. (1985). *Organizational culture and leadership.* San Francisco: Jossey-Bass.

The author emphasizes the leader's role in shaping and creating culture through recruiting and selecting, modeling, storytelling, controlling, and spending time.

Shelton, M. (1989). *The faculty meeting leader's guide.* Kalamazoo: Baker & Barnett.

The author challenges principals to make faculty meetings effective through planning, communicating, securing input, identifying and solving problems, and evaluating meetings. Helpful planning, implementing, and evaluating forms are provided.

Watkins, B. (1992). Universities try electronic format to make meetings more productive. *Chronicle of Higher Education, 16,* 22.

The author discusses the use of E-mail, video conferencing, and brainstorming via computers, rather than holding traditional meetings.

Whitehead, J. (1983). *Tips for chairpersons.* Association of Governing Boards of Universities and Colleges. (ERIC Document Reproduction Service No. 236 970)

The author argues that agenda and background information, as well as reaching consensus rather than deciding by majority vote, are all necessary for successful meetings.

Whitehead, J. (1984). *Improving meeting productivity.* Proceedings of the Southeast Convention of the American Business Communication Association. (ERIC Document Reproduction Service No. 262 402)

The author states that meetings are organizational rituals, which actually waste time; in fact, meetings generally last as long as time is allocated. In contrast to many researchers, the author argues against using agendas because they destroy creativity.

Willings, D., & Chamberlain, N. (1992). Autonomous imagery—A new approach. *Gifted Education International, 8,* 10-15.

The authors examine using autonomous imagery to engender brainstorming in meetings. They suggest starting meetings with "I know this sounds crazy, but . . . ."

Yates, D. (1985). *The politics of management.* San Francisco: Jossey-Bass.

The author dispels the idea of a "perfect leader" and suggests that one's background, whether in law, policy, finances, politics, efficiency, or organizational behavior, shapes one's personal management style. Of particular interest is the analysis of how a staff assistant shapes the leader's opinion of employees.

Yeomans, W. (1985). *1000 things you never learned in business school.* New Jersey: Mentor.

The author discusses why meetings should never be held without a definite purpose and how meetings can be used to advance one's own career by demonstrating knowledge, skills, humor, and astuteness. Anticipating problems, determining possible stances that individuals may take on particular issues, and lining up support for one's position prior to going into a meeting are also covered.